AF399783

DEVELOPING YOUR CAREER STRATEGY

Tips for a brighter professional future

Written by Maïlys Charlier
Translated by Rebecca Neal

DEVELOPING YOUR CAREER STRATEGY

- **Problem:** how can you formulate an effective career plan? What steps can you take to achieve your professional goals?
- **Uses:** developing a career strategy will enable you to make the necessary professional decisions to turn your plans into reality.
- **Professional context:** job search, career change, promotion, skills management, career management.
- **FAQs:**
  - What is a career plan?
  - How can I draw up a career plan in practice?
  - When should I draw up or review my career plan?
  - What tools will enable me to reach my professional objectives?
  - How can I get to know myself better so that I can develop a personalised career plan?
  - How can I develop my professional image?
  - What role does my CV play in my career

strategy?
- ◦ Will a career strategy allow me to accomplish all my objectives?

Virtually all of us have faced the question "Where do you see yourself five years from now?", either during a job interview, as part of an annual performance review, or even during a conversation with friends. We often do not give our answer too much thought, but this question is significant, especially when it comes to work, because our wellbeing is partly dependent on our professional success.

This is especially the case given that it is no simple matter to find a job that is suited to your skills and abilities, progress within your company or embark on a successful career. It all requires careful thought and preparation. Furthermore, given the current economic climate, there is little room for error: job security is not guaranteed and every vacancy attracts legions of candidates.

Which job is right for you? How can you identify your skills? What are your professional goals and how can you get there? These are all useful questions, whether you are happy with your current situation but are looking to progress quickly, are at a dead end in your career or are looking for a career change. No matter what your situation, there are a number of strategies you can implement to reach your goals. Ultimately, your professional success depends on how you manage your career. In 50 minutes, this book will guide you through the different steps you need to follow to develop your career strategy.

EFFECTIVE CAREER MANAGEMENT: THE BASICS

WHY SHOULD YOU DEVELOP A CAREER PLAN?

Are you feeling unfulfilled in your current job? Do you feel as though you are not getting the recognition you deserve? Do you have skills that you are not making the most of at work? Are you struggling to find a job where your expertise can be put to good use?

Nowadays, many of us would like to change jobs, either because our job is not (or is no longer) what we want, or because there is no room for growth at our current company. Other factors can also play a role: an unpleasant atmosphere, the pressure of the current economic situation, short-term contracts, a poor salary or, particularly among younger workers, the desire for new experiences. Consequently, now might be a good time to evaluate your career so far and review your strategy in order to achieve your professional objectives. A career plan can help you to do this. Taking your personality into account and evaluating your skills will give you a better idea of the direction to take your career in.

> "I was a lorry driver for several years, but a bad fall forced me to leave the job. I then started studying logistics in order to become a planning agent. I found a job in concrete logistics in 2007 and began studying chocolate-making at the same time, as this is something I have a real passion for. My original plan was to do it on a freelance basis and then switch to full-time once the chocolate shop got off the ground. In the end, I was laid off from the concrete company in 2011, so I decided to turn my passion into a full-time job earlier than planned and open my handmade chocolate shop. Four years later, I had to move into new premises that were four times bigger – it just goes to show that anything is possible!" (Rita, chocolate-maker at La Chocolaterie du Haut Clocher in Belgium)

Remember that any change at work (career change, new job with more responsibilities, and so on) may have an impact on your personal life. If you used to have more traditional working hours and switch to a new job that needs you to be more flexible, you will have to reorganise your personal life. The same goes for salary: you may end up making less than before. All these factors need to be taken into account when you are devising your career plan.

DRAWING UP YOUR CAREER PLAN

Your career strategy will allow you to put concrete measures in place to get to where you want to go. There are three essential questions to ask yourself:

- Where am I in my career?
- Where do I want to go?
- What can I do to get there?

However, there are very different ways to go about this. For example, the French human resources researcher and professor Jean-Marie Peretti (born in 1946) advises formulating a career plan based on the following questions:

- What roles have I had so far?
- How can I balance my professional life and my personal life?
- What matters most to me? (Company, position, atmosphere, location, working conditions, and so on.)
- What are my strengths and weaknesses when trying to secure a job?
- What steps can I take to reach my goal?

The authors of the book *GRH. Une approche internationale* ("Human Resource Management: An International Approach") outline five steps for determining your career plan:

- analyse your professional history;
- analyse your ambitions, motivations and potential;
- define your professional and career choices;
- identify the means at your disposal;
- implement a strategy and a plan of action to progress towards your objectives.

Identifying your skills

Identifying your skills is the first step in drawing up a career plan. The aim is to know where you stand in the professional world and to highlight your values, knowledge and skills; in other words, everything you picked up during your studies, internships and past jobs. Whether you are a student or a worker, review the past year and make a note of all your successes, in as much detail as possible. Putting everything down on paper will allow you to take a step back and make it easier to analyse your professional profile. These simple rules will help you to identify your skills:

- create a precise account of your experiences by specifying the title of each position and describing the tasks it entailed;
- use action verbs (implement, develop, prepare, direct, and so on) to illustrate your qualities;
- do not leave anything out, even if some elements or areas of expertise do not seem particularly relevant to you.

This will enable you not only to better target the job that suits you, optimise your CV and thus increase your chances of attracting an employer's attention, but also, from a more personal point of view, to identify the qualities you need to acquire or develop in order to reach your career objectives.

Career anchors

According to Edgar Schein (born in 1928), a former professor at the MIT Sloan School of Management, our career paths are determined by a range of "career anchors", meaning the personal values we rely on to make professional choices. They encompass the skills, motivations, principles and attitudes that guide us and give our careers direction and stability. You can use Schein's outline to identify your anchors (it is of course possible to have several anchors). This will make it easier to develop a career strategy and aim for a job that suits you.

Schein's eight career anchors

Technical-functional competence
Do you possess expertise in a particular domain?

Lifestyle
What balance do you want between your professional life and your personal life?

General managerial competence
Are you capable of taking on responsibilities and managing a team?

Pure challenge
Do you perform better when you are facing a challenge?

Autonomy/ independence
Do you need to be given instructions to organise your work?

Service or dedication to a cause
Do you want to fight for a cause that matters to you?

Security/stability
Do you need to feel reassured in terms of your finances?

Entrepreneurial creativity
Do you feel capable of founding and running a business?

Defining your objectives

To determine what you aspire to in your professional future, list your dreams, what motivates you in your career, the jobs you are drawn to and the companies you would like to work for. Next, bring all this information together and look into what specific jobs are best suited to your skills and personal values.

To set feasible objectives, ask yourself well-targeted questions: what skills are employers looking for in the profession I want to pursue? What are the economic trends in the sector I am interested in? Which companies might need my skills? Where do I see myself ten years from now? How do I want my career to develop?

The SMART method is an easy, effective way of setting both short- and long-term objectives.

The SMART method

Specific	Your objectives should be as precise as possible. For example, instead of saying "I want to improve my IT skills", you should set goals like "I want to be able to create a website/run a blog/develop a programme".
Measur- able	You must be able to measure your progress: "I want to have finished my website by the end of the month".
Achiev- able	If you set the bar too high, you will struggle to achieve your aim. Working in stages and progressing step by step will increase your chances of success and keep you motivated.
Realistic	Know that there is a difference between your dreams and reality. Becoming the next Bill Gates is a big ask, but you can gain recognition as an IT specialist by developing your skills in the domain.
Time- bound	If you do not have a deadline, your motivation will wane and you will have no way of determining whether or not you have achieved your objective.

Extra information

Explore growth sectors, where new roles could emerge in the near future. You will have a greater chance of success in these fields than in sectors where the demand for jobs far outstrips supply.

TAKE ACTION TO PROGRESS IN YOUR CAREER

Continuous learning

In his article "Advice for the underemployed class of 2014", Thomas A. Kochan (born in 1947), also a professor at the MIT Sloan School of Management, outlines a series of strategies to optimise your career.

- His first piece of advice is to focus on the things you excel at and to "Be aggressive and creative in putting your skills to work". If your current job does not give you the opportunity to make use of them, find another way of maintaining them: if you are a gifted writer, write for yourself during your free time; if you have a passion for graphic design, offer your services to any friends who might need them.
- Kochan's second point relates to your attitude to your current job. He argues that it is necessary to demonstrate initiative and challenge

yourself on a daily basis. This means that you should not limit yourself to the tasks that form part of your own job, but also offer your services for other projects, even if they go beyond the basic functions of your role.

- Finally, Kochan recommends continuing to acquire new skills and to develop the ones that you already have. He believes that in the current economic climate, jobs are no longer as stable as they once were, so it is best to keep learning in order to be prepared for any nasty surprises. He suggests taking an interest in in-demand professions and "look[ing] at where technology in your profession is going" so that you do not get left behind in your sector.

Your professional skills are one of the keys to success in your career. Without them, you are worth nothing in the eyes of your (potential) employer, so you need to keep honing them throughout your career in accordance with your objectives. For example, if you aspire to a management role, learning how to manage conflicts and developing your leadership skills will be very useful to you. There are a range of training programmes, coaching courses and work placements that can help you to change careers or reach your professional objectives. MOOCs (Massive Open Online Courses) are ideal, because they provide continuous education via distance learning and cover virtually every field, from marketing to accounting to law. It is also possible to follow other education and training courses from the comfort of your own home thanks to e-learning.

The Proactive Career Management Strategy method

The Proactive Career Management Strategy (*Stratégie Proactive de Gestion de Carrière*, or SPGC in French) method, developed by Patrick Daymand, is based on a range of tools and methods which aim to turn skills into added value and allow individuals to achieve their professional goals more easily. The SPGC method involves proposing a well-thought-out project to a company that has the means to make it a reality. In other words, if your dream is to work for a particular company, work out what you could contribute and develop a project in order to convince them that you are indispensable to them. Further information on this method (in French) can be found on the SPGC website (http://spgc-carriere.fr/).

Networking

Building up a substantial list of well-placed contacts is an essential component of professional success. If you have an extensive, high-quality network, you will be able to get in touch with the right people to move your career or your project forward. With this in mind, target experts in your field and make sure that you are on their radar. Taking part in networking events (workshops, trade fairs, seminars, conferences) linked to the sector you are interested in may give you the opportunity to meet people who could help you out in future. Research who will be there in advance, as this will make it easier to have a constructive conversation. The following tips will help you to network more effectively:

- Ask yourself which people it would be useful to form connections with. After this, do not leave your conversations to chance, but establish a plan of action.
- Prepare an introductory sentence that will en-

able you to start a conversation with anyone.
- Prepare so that you can sell yourself in a very short period of time.
- Stay positive, confident and smiling at all times.
- Let the other person speak, show that you are interested in them, pay attention to what they have to say and ask them questions.
- Do not spend all your time with the same person. Cut the conversation short if you need to, thank them for their time and ask for their business card so that you can get in touch with them later on.
- Keep in touch with the people you have spoken to by sending a thank-you email, asking for news from them or asking for information on a specific subject.
- Make the most of social media: you can use it to announce that you are taking part in a particular event, then post photos, tweets and statuses about it. Remember to respond to other people's posts as well.

> "I use networking a lot to develop my business. It's a good way of promoting my chocolate and meeting potential new customers. I go to the event organised by the Chamber of Commerce

every year, and I regularly take part in activities organised by various networks for women in business." (Rita, continued)

Social networks

In our hyperconnected world, social networks play a vital role in our career development. If you have not yet created LinkedIn, Twitter and Facebook accounts (among others), now is the time to put things right. Whether you are embarking on a new project or changing career, these social networks are a valuable source of help.

- **LinkedIn.** This is the first site you should consider, because it is used for the specific purpose of creating professional networks and is therefore a fundamental tool in the world of work. Join specialised groups for the sector you want to break into and take part in discussions about subjects related to your area of expertise. Make sure you keep your profile, and particularly your skills and experiences, up to date, as employers regularly consult LinkedIn. You can also use the site to research potential customers or partners.

- **Viadeo.** This social network is very similar to LinkedIn, since it is used primarily for professional purposes and can help you to develop your personal brand. The site is packed with potential customers and enables you to join discussions between professionals on very specific subjects.
- **Twitter.** This site also has its uses, but you must make sure you approach it intelligently. Tweeting a constant stream of useless, frivolous information risks making you look unprofessional and undermining your credibility. Select your key topics, tweet no more than once or twice a day and make judicious use of hashtags. Feel free to also consult the many job advertisements that are published on Twitter. Finally, when you go to a professional event, tweet about it and follow the expert guests.
- **Facebook.** This social network is used primarily for leisure, but can also be useful for career management. Job postings circulate constantly, and there are a wide range of professional pages or groups that could be useful to you. To communicate effectively on Facebook, start by creating a professional

page and sharing it with as many people as possible via your personal account and other media (website, email signature, and so on). Talk about it to your friends, colleagues and acquaintances. Update your page regularly by posting photos and videos, and communicate with your followers and ask their opinion. Set up a posting schedule to avoid losing track of your content and to make sure that you have enough material. You can get more likes by linking your Google+ (Google's social network) account to your Facebook page: showing up in the popular search engine will help you to attract more followers.

Potential pitfalls

While social networks can be helpful, they also have their downsides and should be used with caution. If you give away too many details about your personal life, you risk losing control of your image. You should also avoid compromising photos, political opinions and tendentious comments. Furthermore, overly commercial posts tend to be less successful with Facebook users. Instead, opt for a more original or humorous approach, as people will be more likely to remember it.

Mastering these social networks can boost your career by helping you to:

- reach a wider audience and increase customer loyalty;
- increase traffic to your website (page views or hits);
- increase your visibility and therefore become more widely known;
- create a genuine community around a project;
- appear higher in search engine results.

Personal branding

If you want a productive, successful career, you need to stand out from the crowd, strengthen your image and build a personal brand that you will maintain throughout your career. Personal branding, which was first defined in 1997 by the American author and management expert Tom Peters (born in 1942), involves turning yourself into a product to be marketed. To do this, you need to come up with a visual identity and highlight the things that make you stand out.

Once you have done this, it is up to you to promote your personal brand on your CV, your website, your social media accounts, your blog and your business card. Running a blog is highly recommended, because this will allow you to develop and showcase your image. However, personal brands are also built in real life, when you meet other people. Make sure you stay true to your brand with all the people you encounter at conferences and training courses, and to hand out business cards here and there.

TOP TIPS

- **Ask yourself the right questions.** Who are you? What sector do you want to work in? What are your strengths and weaknesses? What opportunities do you have? What are you afraid of? How do you see the future? What are your tasks and responsibilities in your current role? What are your short- and long-term goals? How can you accomplish them? What are your priorities? How can you balance your professional life and your personal life? What is your ideal job? Do you have the necessary skills for it? Knowing yourself well is essential to avoid picking the wrong career path.
- **Formulate your career plan as soon as possible.** This will help you to see your professional development more clearly and to make the right decisions at the right time. You can of course adapt it if your objectives change.
- **Get more experience.** This will make you more qualified. There are a number of ways of doing this: changing job regularly (every two to four years) within the same company, get-

ting involved in unusual projects, or starting a job in a different company (in terms of sector, customers, size, and so on).

- **Put together a portfolio.** Portfolios are a requirement in some specific professions, such as modelling or photography, but they can also be useful in other sectors. Compiling your professional documents will allow you to showcase your skills and to have an example of your achievements to hand.
- **Stay informed.** How and where (newspapers, social media, and so on) do not matter that much, but reading up on your job and your sector every day is essential to stay up to date with the latest developments and avoid falling behind.
- **Find the training course that is right for you.** There are a range of training programmes that can help you to develop a career plan that is suited to your needs. Other courses will allow you to develop skills that will be useful later on in your career. Do not forget to include them on your CV.
- **Do not neglect internships.** While it is not pleasant or even always possible to work for free, an internship will give you skills and

experience that will help you later on in your career. Furthermore, it may provide you with further opportunities and even a permanent job afterwards. Finally, internships will allow you to make valuable contacts.

- **Make the most of all your experiences.** Every experience, even short-term contracts and temporary jobs, will give you skills that you can showcase in your CV, in your cover letter, on your website or even in person, for example during an interview. Similarly, skills you have developed outside work can be an asset, but you have to find the right way of framing and describing them.
- **Avoid job-hopping.** If you are constantly leaving your job for greener pastures, you will not give yourself time to acquire new skills.

FAQS

WHAT IS A CAREER PLAN?

A career plan is a long-term strategic plan which involves anticipating your professional development. It will allow you to change direction in your career or to get your professional life off to a strong start thanks to tools that you can use to reach your professional goals. You need to start by analysing your professional identity (skills, experiences, aims, and so on) before devising the right career strategy for you.

HOW CAN I DRAW UP A CAREER PLAN IN PRACTICE?

You should formulate your career strategy methodically, or you risk hitting a roadblock before you even get started. To do this, work through the steps outlined in the diagram below:

The stages in drawing up your career strategy

> **Set deadlines**

> **Use various tools to create your personal brand**

> **Network effectively**

> **Establish a career plan in line with your skills, objectives and career path**

> **Evaluate your skills and objectives in order to select the right career path**

> **Identify your personality type** (What are your motivations, values, qualities and objectives?)

> **Analyse your professional journey so far** (What are your skills, experiences and achievements?)

WHEN SHOULD I DRAW UP OR REVIEW MY CAREER PLAN?

- When you have completed your studies and it is time to look for a job, it is a good idea to start by drawing up a career plan (which will no doubt change repeatedly over time). This will enable you to avoid wasting too much time and energy applying for jobs that are not right for you.

* If you are at a job that has not felt right for some time, you are unfulfilled or you feel that something is missing, it is time to review your career plan and change direction.

WHAT TOOLS WILL ENABLE ME TO REACH MY PROFESSIONAL OBJECTIVES?

Networking is a way of establishing contacts in your professional sector. You can develop your network by taking part in events linked to your job (workshops, trade fairs, conferences, and so on), meeting key figures, handing out business cards, talking to potential partners (suppliers, sales representatives, customers, sponsors, and so on) and being active on social media. Social networks, in particular LinkedIn and Viadeo, which are more focused on the professional world, can help you to find a job or develop your career. They will also allow you to work on your personal brand. Posting quality content will increase your chances of going viral and boosting your reputation by reaching as many people as possible.

HOW CAN I GET TO KNOW MYSELF BETTER SO THAT I CAN DEVELOP A PERSONALISED CAREER PLAN?

Some questionnaires, such as the How, Where, What test and the Myers-Briggs Type Indicator (MBTI), can help you here. The How, Where, What test is useful when you are looking for a job, as it will show you whether your method is as effective as it could be. The MBTI is more personal and will help you to determine your professional profile, your main personality traits, your strengths and your weaknesses. You can try out both tests in the Over to you section of this guide.

HOW CAN I DEVELOP MY PROFESSIONAL IMAGE?

The first step towards developing and consolidating your brand image is to identify your skills and define your objectives. Once you have done this, you will find it easier to create a visual identity that feels right for you and allows you to stand out from your competitors. The next step is to broadcast this image using all the tools you have at your disposal: social media, networking, business cards, blog, website, during conferences and training sessions, and so on. The main ingredient in any effective brand image is authenticity: people will trust you more if you do not pretend to be perfect.

WHAT ROLE DOES MY CV PLAY IN MY CAREER STRATEGY?

Do not neglect your CV: it is your professional passport, and provides proof of your skills and experiences. It is constantly evolving, and you should keep updating it and adapt it to the position you are applying for. To create the ideal CV for the job you want, put yourself in your future employer's shoes, ask yourself what skills and qualities they are looking for, and draw attention to these in your CV. However, if your new career is very different from your previous experience, mention it at the start of your CV and explain why you want to change career. Try to make your CV stand out to attract the attention of your future employer, while making sure that you adhere to the conventional structure (your contact information, qualifications, experiences and skills) and that you are concise as possible. Do not leave out any training or professional experiences, as they all contribute to an overview of qualities and skills which are essential for your future employer.

WILL A CAREER STRATEGY ALLOW ME TO ACCOMPLISH ALL MY OBJECTIVES?

A good career strategy will help you to move closer to your aims and select the tools you need to get there. The rest is up to you!

OVER TO YOU

SKILLS ASSESSMENTS

You can identify your skills more easily and work out what direction to take for the next phase of your career by assessing all your work experience (internships, training, student jobs) and jobs so far in separate documents. If you stayed with the same company for a long time but had different roles, use a separate page for each one. Make a note of the things you learned (expertise, technical skills, and so on) and your responsibilities. Use the same system for your personal activities (sport and leisure) and record the qualities you need for them. This exercise will provide you with answers to several questions: what profession are my skills suited to? What roles in particular? What type of company might need someone like me? What role would I excel in?

THE HOW, WHERE, WHAT TEST

As its name suggests, the How, Where, What test comprises three simple questions:

- **How?** What techniques are you using in your job search? How do you behave during a job interview? What tools are you using to reach your objectives?
- **Where?** What professions are you considering for your career? Organise them by role and by sector.
- **What?** This involves identifying your skills, interests and personality traits.

This test will allow you to check how well you know the steps to find a job (How), how clear your target is (Where) and how good you are at assessing your situation (What).

THE MYERS-BRIGGS TYPE INDICATOR (MBTI)

The MBTI is a psychological evaluation tool which can be used to determine your profile, your strengths, your weaknesses and the types of jobs or sectors that could suit you. It comprises a series of questions about your nature and the way you behave in your private life and in your work. There are two possible answers to each question, and users choose the one that they identify with the most. You can add nuance to your answers with the help of six boxes to show how much you agree with each statement. Tests inspired by the MBTI are freely available online, but the only officially approved version can be found on the OPP website. The following table gives you some examples of statements, but to find out your personality type you will need to take the full test.

I prefer quiet environments and thinking alone.	0					I prefer being active and interacting with people.
I prefer thinking about a new topic alone, then telling other people what I think.						I prefer discussing and debating a new subject as part of a group.
I listen to other people's opinions to make decisions.						I make decisions without asking other people for their input.
I like meeting new people.						I like being alone or with someone I know well.
I do not spend a lot of time focusing on my thoughts or feelings.						I find it easy to talk about my thoughts or feelings.
I speak more than I listen.						I listen more than I speak.

I prefer concrete or real subjects.						I prefer abstract or theoretical subjects.
I prefer to focus on the present and on what is happening.						I prefer to focus on the future and on what could happen.
I make decisions based on factual information.						I make decisions based on my beliefs and feelings.
I consider myself a sensitive person.						I consider myself a rational person.
When a problem arises, my main concern is whether or not it is really a problem.						When a problem arises, my main concern is whether or not it is important.
I can adapt to change and I like to keep all my options open.						I prefer routine and knowing what might happen in advance.

FURTHER READING

BIBLIOGRAPHY

- 1819. (No date) *Bien réseauter: comment faire ?* [Online]. [Accessed 3 October 2017]. Available from: <http://www.1819.be/fr/marketing-vente-e-commerce/faire-de-la-promotion-et-la-publicite/bien-reseauter-comment-faire>

- Agence France Entrepreneur. (2016) *Utiliser les réseaux sociaux pour communiquer et prospecter sur le web.* [Online]. [Accessed 3 October 2017]. Available from: <https://www.afecreation.fr/pid12268/les-reseaux-sociaux.html?espace=3>

- Alis, D., Besseyre des Horts, C-H., Chevalier, F., Fabi, B. and Peretti, J-M. (2001) *GRH. Une approche internationale.* 3rd edition. Louvain-la-Neuve: De Boeck.

- ANPE. (2006) *Comment identifier ses savoir-faire et ses qualités.* [Online]. [Accessed 3 October 2017]. Available from: <http://www.metiers-ducommerce.fr/pdf/comment_identifier_ses_savoir-faire_et_qualites.pdf>

- CadresOnline. (No date) *Définir ses objectifs professionnels ou comment s'auto-évaluer en prenant du recul sur sa vie professionnelle.*

[Online]. [Accessed 3 October 2017]. Available from: <http://www.cadresonline.com/conseils/coaching/cv-lettres-entretiens/preparer-entretien-dembauche/detail/article/definir-ses-objectifs-professionnels-ou-comment-sauto-evaluer-en-prenant-du-recul-sur-sa-vie-prof.html>

- Equipaje. (No date) *Ancres de carrière.* [Online]. [Accessed 3 October 2017]. Available from: <http://www.equipaje.fr/fr/books/guide-de-lemploi-letranger/ancres-de-carriere>

- Guérin, O. (2012) Valoriser son image tout au long de sa carrière, la stratégie gagnante. *Journal du Net.* [Online]. [Accessed 3 October 2017]. Available from: <http://www.journaldunet.com/management/expert/51994/valoriser-son-image-tout-au-long-de-sa-carriere--la-strategie-gagnante.shtml>

- Jobat.be. (2014) *Prêt à changer de carrière ? Faites le point en 4 étapes.* [Online]. [Accessed 3 October 2017]. Available from: <http://www.jobat.be/fr/articles/pret-a-changer-de-carriere-faites-le-point-en-4-etapes/>

- Kochan, T. A. (2014) Advice for the underemployed class of 2014. *Fortune.* [Online]. [Accessed 3 October 2017]. Available from: <http://fortune.com/2014/05/20/advice-for-the-underemployed-class-of-2014/>

- Longour, M. (No date) Premier emploi : bien définir son objectif professionnel. *Réussir ma vie.* [Online]. [Accessed 3 October 2017]. Available from:

<https://www.reussirmavie.net/Premier-emploi-bien-definir-son-objectif-professionnel_a1131.html>

- Mon Incroyable Job. (2014) *Gestion de carrière selon Darwin, « Mooc » & formation continue de chez soi.* [Online]. [Accessed 3 October 2017]. Available from: <http://www.monincroyablejob.com/gestion-carriere-selon-darwin-mooc-formation-continue-chez-soi/>

- Préaux, C. (2014) Le networking pour les nuls : 10 astuces. *Références.* [Online]. [Accessed 3 October 2017]. Available from: <https://references.lesoir.be/article/le-networking-pour-les-nuls-10-astuces/>

- Qadeer, S. (2015) Comment trouver un emploi ? Quelques stratégies de carrière à l'intention des nouveaux arrivants. *Etablissement.org.* [Online]. [Accessed 3 October 2017]. Available from: <https://etablissement.org/ontario/emploi/trouver-un-emploi/recherche-d-emploi/comment-trouver-un-emploi-quelques-strategies-de-carriere-a-l-intention-des-nouveaux-arrivants/>

- Reconversion Professionnelle. (No date) *Réussir sa reconversion professionnelle.* [Online]. [Accessed 3 October 2017]. Available from: <https://www.reconversionprofessionnelle.org/>

- Stepstone. (No date) Changement de carrière : comment donner une nouvelle orientation à votre carrière ? [Online]. [Accessed 3 October 2017].

Available from: <http://www.stepstone.be/
Conseils-de-Carriere/Trucs-astuces/changement-
de-carriere-comment-donner-une-nouvelle-orien-
tation-a-votre-carriere.cfm>

- Talents & Carrière. (No date) *Bilan Stratégie de carrière.* [Online]. [Accessed 3 October 2017]. Available from: <http://www.talents-carriere.fr/prestations/bilan-strategie-de-carriere/>

ADDITIONAL SOURCES

- Casnocha, B. and Hoffman, R. (2013) *The Start-up of You: Adapt to the Future, Invest in Yourself, and Transform Your Career.* New York: Random House.

- Fléron, B. (2017) *Personal Branding – Market Yourself!* Trans. Lunt, E. Brussels: Plurilingua Publishing.

- Fléron, B. (2017) *Using the Myers-Briggs Type Indicator.* Trans. Lunt, E. Brussels: Plurilingua Publishing.

- Spies, N. (2017) *Job Seeking on Social Media.* Trans. Neal, R. Brussels: Plurilingua Publishing.

50MINUTES.com

IMPROVE YOUR GENERAL KNOWLEDGE

IN A BLINK OF AN EYE !

www.50minutes.com

Although the editor makes every effort to verify the accuracy of the information published, 50Minutes. com accepts no responsibility for the content of this book.

www.50minutes.com

Ebook EAN: 9782808000390

Paperback EAN: 9782808000406

Legal Deposit: D/2017/12603/447

Cover: © Primento

Digital conception by Primento, the digital partner of publishers.